SOCIAL MEDIA HANDBOOK

A Cultural E-volution

What you should know about social networking: history *and* mystery

Ver. 1

Helen Gallagher
Author: *Release Your Writing*

You are viewing Ver. 1, updated: January, 2010

Portions previously published as *The Mysterious World of Web 2.0,* by Helen Gallagher

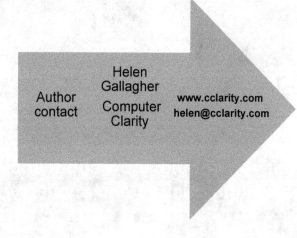

Author contact

Helen Gallagher
Computer Clarity

www.cclarity.com
helen@cclarity.com

Contents

7 Introduction

9 *Social Media Handbook*: Part One
15 Social media usage statistics
16 Web 2.0 History
30 Children online usage
35 Tagging
42 Benefits of Web 2.0
45 About Facebook
49 About LinkedIn
51 About Twitter
54 About YouTube

58 *Social Media Handbook*: Part Two
59 Step 1: Create an account
60 Step 2: Privacy
61 Step 3: Communication
63 Step 4: Networking
65 Step 5: Marketing
70 Computing Chaos?

73 Reader's note pages

Social Media Handbook
explores the debate over Web 2.0

About the book:

Social Media Handbook provides an overview of how Web 2.0 came about and how its changed. I ponder what it means to us as individuals. Also called social networking, Web 2.0 is a new phase of the internet: reaching out to web users for a shared experience, rather than delivery of static web pages or the one-way commentary on most sites.

Corporations are in billion-dollar bidding wars to own these online services, because the users represent massive potential revenue for advertisers.

But what do these sites do? Who has time to use them, and what effect will they have on literacy and culture? This is a worldwide issue that has significant effect on what children are doing in school, how they learn, and what they will become.

The old "information superhighway" was a one-way street. If we wanted something we went to a web site and retrieved it. Today it's all about a collaborative, interactive social networking experience, for better or worse.

Social Media Handbook was published both in print and in ebook format specifically so the ebook can be updated as the fast-paced web world changes. Purchase information for both versions is available at the author's web site, Computer Clarity, www.cclarity.com

Helen Gallagher

Author contact: Helen@cclarity.com
© 2010, Helen Gallagher

THE MYSTERIOUS WORLD OF WEB 2.0

First there was the **Internet** in the 1960s.

Then, with the invention of hypertext, the **worldwide web** became a graphical interface for internet content in 1991.

Web 2.0 is the umbrella term for all that has come since then... Using the web not as a static way to deliver web content, but as an integrated, participatory way to socialize, involve and engage viewers, contributing web content we hope is worth the reader's time and attention.

Social media is where we are now, using the organized aggregation and delivery of integrated text, audio, and video. The social element comes about because people started to email each other interesting links, then services like Facebook got people to sign up, have a page to post what they like, and draw others to the site, with exponential growth unseen in human history.

Acronym Madness: A new shorthand, used by people typing on thumb pads and cell phones. Very common now as abbreviations and typing quick Twitter messages, which are limited to 140 characters.

AFAIK As far as I know	NM Nothing much
BBL Be back later	NOYB None of your business
B4N Bye for now	NP No problem
BRB Be right back	NRN No reply needed
BTW By the way	OHM Oh my God
CUL8R See you later	OTP On the phone
F2F Face-to-face	PMFJI Pardon me for jumping in
FWIW For what it's worth	
GOI Get over it	POS Parents over shoulder
IMHO In my humble opinion	POV Point of view
IOH I'm outta here	ROTFL Rolling on the floor laughing
IOW In other words	
IRL In real life	RUOK Are you okay?
ITS I told you so	TIA Thanks in advance
KIT Keep in touch	TMI or 2MI Too much information
LOL Laughing out loud	
LTL Lets talk later	TTFN Ta Ta for now
LTNS Long time no see	TTYL Talk to you later
	UKW You know who

You'll find a huge acronym list at:	www.netlingo.com/emailsh.cfm

All web links current and verified 12/18/09

SOCIAL MEDIA HANDBOOK
Part One

Where it began

What it does

History

The big picture

But what about blogs?

Blogs are not covered in this first edition of *Social Media Handbook* because they are a different communication vehicle.

Blogs are more purposeful, usually chronological and focused on a topic, written with a specific tone.

. A blogging guide will be published in Spring, 2010.

Where it began...

New things come about because there's room for them in society, because what we already have isn't perfect, and because there's big money to be made. Hence Web 2.0, the second generation of the Internet, where static web pages are replaced by interactive sites, with content contributed by users and shared instantly with the public.

This social networking or social media is the new face of the internet: reaching out to web users for a shared experience, rather than delivery of static web pages or the one-way commentary on most blogs.

Things change fast in technology. MySpace used to have 80 percent of the social networking market. Then thousands of MySpace users jumped over to Facebook, and tomorrow may hop over to the next new thing. What will it be? Maybe Twiddle, Doofus, or another time-drain...or whatever else comes along. As of this writing, Hi5.com has come along, the newest kid on the block.

The story doesn't end there. We consider the effect these social sites have on creating buzz for a hit movie and celebrity-chasing. The power of Twitter and Facebook to sway public opinion is startling, and there's great concern about this growing focus away from trained journalists to consumers creating their own news, unfiltered.

What it does...

Web 2.0 provides a place where anyone can create a public profile and build a personal network to connect to like-minded online users. Web 2.0 sites include MySpace, Facebook, and Flickr (which had 3,842 photos uploaded in the last minute, as I write this). Typical content on social media sites might be text, chat, video, and personalized pages to track friends, events, and interests.

But what do these sites do? Who has time to use them, and what effect will they have on literacy and culture? This is a worldwide issue that has significant effect on what children are doing in school, how they learn, and what they will become.

Today, web use is all about a collaborative, interactive social networking experience, for better or worse.

According to Pew Internet & American Life Project:

46% of online American adults 18 and older use a social networking site like MySpace, Facebook or LinkedIn, up from 8% in February 2005.

65% of teens 12-17 use online social networks as of Feb 2008, up from 58% in 2007 and 55% in 2006.

http://www.pewinternet.org/Infographics/Growth-in-Adult-SNS-Use-20052009.aspx

Web 2.0 is more of an attitude than technology. Newspapers also presume an inner awareness of vernacular, language and meaning. Arriving here from another country, would you understand this newspaper headline? "Big 3, UAW at critical juncture." Is it referring to airplanes, sports teams? That's strange language for automakers and a union, but it creeps into common usage and becomes the norm.

So today we talk of blogs, YouTube, Wiki's, Facebook and tweets, all of which open doors for people to share and collaborate. Early sites developed for photo and music sharing proved millions of people would use these online portals, and today it has spread to people sharing comments, opinions, photos, friends, and poking each other all day on sites like Twitter.com where you tell friends what are you doing.

As fortunes are made, and investors reap profits, it's likely Web 2.0 and its social media sites will form the basis for a new kind of online life, blending reality and fantasy, truth and nonsense, leaving it to the web user to discern the value.

To avoid wasting time or straying too far, learn to recognize sites with contributed content and sites that aggregate popular information. Stick with those that place restrictions on input, rather than a web community. Those ad-hoc sites may be filled with popular opinion, not necessarily based in fact.

And who knows, maybe some day instead of draining our focus and productivity, these sites will benefit society, providing better communication services for those with disabilities, creating more efficient processes for home-based workers, or even making people smarter.

Could it one day represent the world's largest fact-filled database? We'll see...

Until then, we're watching people use massive internet resources to display videos of a bicycling dog, baby hippos, and an unending stream of drunken karaoke singers. Let's find out why . . .

Social Networking Usage Statistics:
from Pew Internet & American Life Project

- 89 percent of adults surveyed use their online profile to keep up with friends
- 57 percent use their profile to make plans with friends
- 49 percent use them to make new friends
- 51 percent of social network users have two or more online profiles
- 43 percent have only one online profile
- Over 53 million Americans used the internet to publish their thoughts, post pictures, share files, etc.
- 85 percent have ever used search engines
- Only sending and reading email outranks search engine queries as an online activity.

Pew data gathered in national phone survey (November 19 to December 20, 2008 among 2,253 Americans, including 1,650 internet users. Margin of error=+/- 3%

http://www.pewinternet.org/Reports/2009/Adults-and-Social-Network-Websites.aspx?r=1

Web 2.0 has become more pervasive than most of the experts thoughts. A few years ago, more teens than adults embraced this technology. Now things are different:

The internet takes on a different shape today. New ideas catch on because there's room for them... and because what we have already isn't perfect.... and because there's money to be made.

Hence Web 2.0, the second generation :

A place where a web user can create a public profile and build a personal network to connect to like-minded online users. So use of Web 2.0 is more of an attitude than technology.

This all seems successful and fun, so what's the problem? It is nearly inescapable today, but will it be gone tomorrow? Is social networking worth your time?

Explore the many ways successful entrepreneurs are working with social media sites such as Facebook, Twitter, and LinkedIn, to sustain their visibility and add credibility. As part of a professional platform, these avenues can open doors, put your work in front of the right people, and keep you connected with the larger world of publishing.

When Tim Berners-Lee first invented the graphical interface for the web in 1991, he designed it as a device to allow people to work together, using hypertext documents to combine information from different sources. Little did he know what that shared ability would become today.

You'll find fascinating information on Tim Berners-Lee here:
http://www.w3.org/People/Berners-Lee/FAQ.html

In late 2007, at Michigan State University, Jane Briggs-Bunting, director of the school of journalism, was in the news for sharing her views of this virtual world. She states:

"The freshmen enrolling at our colleges and universities today have grown up surrounded by technology– and it's just a tool to them... Many have created their own identities in virtual worlds like Second Life, where no one knows if they are 12 or 45... They are impatient, energetic, live on their cells and text their friends constantly. Frankly, most of them don't get what we do. They are news consumers, but have no brand loyalty."

So, maybe you're asking…

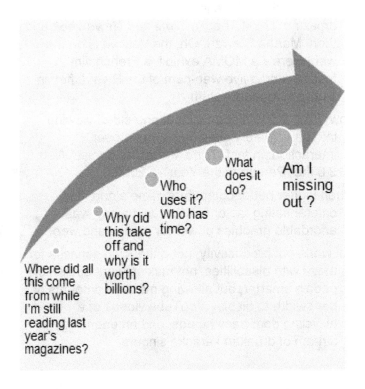

What does it do?

Am I missing out ?

Who uses it? Who has time?

Why did this take off and why is it worth billions?

Where did all this come from while I'm still reading last year's magazines?

Remember where we started?

When we first used the internet, everything was amazing: Look! There's *Time* and *Newsweek* and then, Martha Stewart. Oh, the Vatican is on the web! Here's a MOMA exhibit, a French film festival, and a live web-cam of the River Liffey in Dublin. Wonderful stuff!

Now, Web 2.0 has spun all that one-sided viewing into participatory sites built around peer interaction. In fact, *Time Magazine* named Web 2.0 the "Person of the Year" in 2006.

When bigger better computers came along, the differentiating factor they brought along was affordable graphics power for games and web.

Not work, not productivity, not enhancing services for those with disabilities, not making work easier, or people smarter, but allowing massive amounts of bandwidth to display YouTube videos of a bicycling dog, baby hippos, and an unending stream of drunken karaoke singers.

Where did this come from?

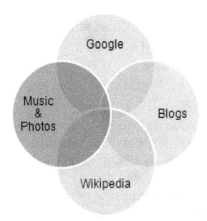

This is not all bad, and it is not all new. From my observations, tracking the industry over the past decade, it likely started with the launch of internet music download sites. They, and popular tools like Google, were probably the forerunners. They made information available for free and people flocked to these sites, beyond all expectations. Of course, advertising dollars quickly followed.

TV and newspapers also presume an inner awareness of vernacular, language and meaning that is lost on many people.

So the Web 2.0 sites and their twisted use of language, spelling and grammar are probably here to stay.

Citizen journalism is becoming common, with people on the street suddenly broadcasting breaking news on CNN. In a 60-second clip, you might hear one witness say "three men ran from the bank shooting guns," and another say "one man walked out, and no shots were fired." So is this news? Is it journalism?

On television, we're asked to text-message our vote on the best American Idol performer, rate the president's speech, and decide whether a criminal should be set free.

Blogs, Google, and Wikipedia, the online encyclopedia opened doors for people to share online. Open-source technology lets anyone do anything. What the photo and music sharing pioneers proved is that millions of people would actually spend time chasing these ideas. The Web 2.0 sites are interactive, not passive, so there are more eyeballs looking at ads, spending money on products and services advertised. Those dollars fuel even more venture capital funding for sites and spin-offs.

Even consumer magazines and newspapers are moving toward social interaction with blogs, restaurant and movie reviews, and dozens of other sites they own, geared to specific demographics, dividing their readers/subscriber into niche segments. These publications stream continuous updates to Facebook and Twitter, changing "news" from a once daily event to a non-stop flow.

We hear a great deal in the media about every fad, including these:

> Facebook
> LinkedIn
> MySpace
> Twitter
> YouTube

But they represent just a small sampling of over 100 popular Web 2.0 sites as of this writing. And remember, worldwide, there are millions of people using sites developed in other countries and used in other languages than English.

Tomorrow we might wake up to a new name, and a new millionaire investor who makes it big by creating something people want and making it available free.

(All sites above end in .com, since they are commercial ventures).

Meme …a little history

Origin: Greek word used in genetics: mimeme, meaning "something imitated."

A **meme** comprises a unit of cultural information, the building block of cultural evolution or diffusion that propagates from one mind to another analogous to the way in which a gene propagates from one organism to another as a unit of genetic information and of biological evolution.

Biologist and evolutionary theorist Richard Dawkins coined the term *meme* in 1976. He gave these examples: tunes, catch-phrases, beliefs, clothing fashions, and the technology of building arches.

100 years before that, Mark Twain in *A Literary Nightmare*, describes his encounter with a jingle so "catchy" that it plays over and over in his mind until he finally sings it out loud and infects others (also known as an earworm).

But it's not all bad

Chat groups, forums, online list-servs covering
medical issues, finances, small business,
parenting groups – those are all examples of
social engineering. People are free to participate,
share information and help others with what they
learned.

Many groups share photo albums online and over 70
percent of web users reach out to Wikipedia for
information and use Google as a verb.

Social Media = Big $$$

Microsoft paid $240 million for a 1.6 percent share of the social networking site in October, 2007. Facebook now has over 350 million users. This company did not even exist until 2004.

"Facebook ads," is a system designed to allow advertisers to customize their marketing for specific users on the site. Some of these advertisers include heavy-hitters like major consumer electronics and media companies.

Facebook users now have greater privacy concerns than just who's looking at their pictures and profile.

As this book went to press, Twitter announced it received $25 million in funding to make all that Twitter chatter searchable. *Business Week* reports this cash infusion will make three-year old Twitter profitable for the first time. User posts will be searchable on Google and Bing, but no word yet on how many users will object to having their casual short messages archived online for the world to see.

www.businessweek.com/technology/content/dec2009/tc20091220_549879.htm

A sampling of social media sites used by adults & teens

Digg, Furl, Stumbleupon Reddit.com: learn what people are clicking on.	Wikipedia, wikimedia wiktionary (collaborative websites).
Instant messaging and text messages result in LoudTalk and Twitter. Twitter asks "What are you doing?"	Technorati: a blog search engine. New programs search only social network sites.
My Space once held 85 percent of the market. Facebook was restricted to school users until Sept. 2006. Now it's larger than MySpace.	You Tube: millions of audio/video files posted by companies as well as amateurs.
Others: Second Life Photo sites, such as Ofoto, Flickr, Snapfish	Yap provides voice-to-text translation services for mobile phones. Users can say anything they like and Yap will send a text copy to anyone of their contacts.

There is a large concern that what is on the web becomes vernacular made up by "a boy in his bedroom," that we have no backup for this enormous online world and it literally has no basis in reality. Yet fortunes are made, investors reap profits, and the spiral continues.

Because users can create any content, you have to make sure Facebook pages you visit are genuine. Conversely, it means you can also create a Facebook page for your favorite celebrity, charity, or book group.

When we later discuss set-up details, you'll see you can create a Facebook page that is not open to the public, and can restrict your page like a private users group.

Children's online activities

Facebook, originally started as a way for students to keep in touch, was primarily used by teen and pre-teen children. Use was restricted only to those with a .edu email address, meaning school-age children, through college.

As a result of the early use among children, there was great controversy about the content, about peer-pressure, and extreme bullying.

Now that adults make up such a large percentage the age range and types of content visible to both children and adults has blended into some level of societal norms.

Social networking:
The effects on children

Potential benefits	Likely Risks
• Reinforce friendships	• Cyber-bullies
• Expand socialization skills	• Danger: flirting, hidden identities, fraud, mob psychology
• Make plans	
• Private email	• Dumbing down of culture
• Users surveyed:	
• 46 percent use daily	• Illiteracy

As an author and computer consultant, I don't learn this from kids on the street, but from Business Week, Forbes, Microsoft research labs, the Wall Street Journal, and the Macarthur Foundation which recently invested $50 million to learn more about the effects of this social networking craze.

One example of a social media site that seems to have fallen popularity is SecondLife.com, where users create a fantasy personality, buy and sell goods with fake currency, called "Linden dollars," and build an entire virtual identity with avatars. We haven't heard anything about SecondLife in many months, so it may be another form of social media that's on the way out.

Pew Internet research shows generational differences in social media users, and the particular activities they pursue.

For example, 65 percent of teens use social networking sites, compared to only 35 percent of adults.

Older users dominate in use of online resources for health information, purchasing, online banking and getting government or religious information.

*

Excerpted from source:
www.pewinternet.org/Infographic
s/Generational-differences-in-
online-activities.aspx

Making sense of it all…

➢ Recognize sites with contributed content and sites that aggregate popular information may not be as accurate as traditional media.

➢ Remember the differences between journalism and opinion.

➢ Use "tags" to filter out the noise

➢ Ads on sites and blogs give you an idea of who is funding the site and what audience they target.

➢ Learn how to start, maintain your profile, or your privacy, and how to benefit from social media sites. Some of the best uses are among creative arts teams, grassroots organizations, neighborhood communities, business networking, affinity groups.

Tagging

Tags, similar to keywords, are a type of weighted text. They were intended as a way for people to organize their research. They quickly became almost cultish, worn like a badge that indicates the popularity of certain terms in online searches.

Like folklore, these tagging social experiences are defined as **Folksonomy**, defined in dictionary.com as: "a type of classification system for online content, created by an individual user who tags information with freely chosen keywords; also, the cooperation of a group of people to create such a classification system."

See http://en.wikipedia.org/wiki/Tag_cloud for a discussion on accuracy and meaning.

And is online content true? It was always suspect, but now we have to hold it to a higher standard. When "anyone" can contribute material that may or may not be accurate, we lose the journalistic filter.

Even Wikipedia, the online collaborative encyclopedia says so, about it's own material:

"It is in the nature of an ever-changing work like Wikipedia that, while some articles are of the highest quality of scholarship, others are admittedly complete rubbish. We are fully aware of this."

Source:

Ten things you may not know about Wikipedia

http://en.wikipedia.org/wiki/Wikipedia:10_things_you_did_not_know_about_Wikipedia

Tagging

Press release tags as example of using tags to filter the subset of information you want. This sample would quickly let you focus on PR announcements related to "launches" and it tells you they don't have as much depth about "shopping sites." This helps you find what you're looking for quicker.

Sample of a tag cloud

abuse academy analysis announces approval available bank banking becomes books business california center commercial competitive compliance conference contest cut day deal deploys direct edcomm estate firm first gold group have home how industry internet invited latest launches learning major marketing medical microsoft million mobile need new now online partner planners police present product professionals property pyratecon real receives reports rocsearch sales school series services shopping site software talk test their traffic training voip website year

Aggregated filters

The New York Times filters the amount of interest in topics, making it easy for you to cut through the clutter and find what is most popular. Note the popularity of a topic may not be most relevant to you, but garners the most interest among readers.

MOST POPULAR

E-MAILED   BLOGGED   SEARCHED

1. Age of Riches: Hedge Funds and Private Equity Alter Career Calculus
2. Do We Really Know What Makes Us Healthy?
3. Ayn Rand's Literature of Capitalism
4. Op-Ed Contributor: This Is Your (Father's) Brain on Drugs
5. Alabama Plan Brings Out Cry of Resegregation
6. The DNA Age: Cancer Free at 33, but Weighing a Mastectomy
7. Paul Krugman: Sad Alan's Lament
8. Parrot Power: Alex Wanted a Cracker, but Did He Want One?
9. Japanese Housewives Sweat in Secret as Markets Reel
10. Argentine Church Faces 'Dirty War' Past

Go to Complete List »

The New York Times

A sample tag cloud from Wikipedia,
depicting frequency of
words related to the term Web 2.0

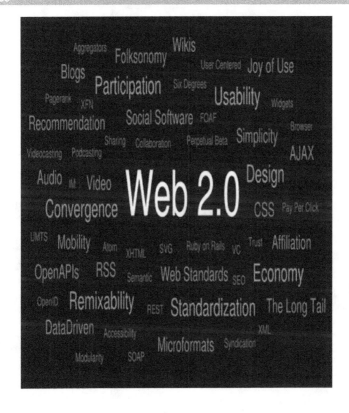

A useful tag cloud depicting world population. In the original file, each name is clickable, to drill down to further details.

Effects on society

A BBC News report on September 11, 2007 states an employment law firm studied 3,500 UK companies and projected 233 million hours are lost every month as a result of employees "wasting time" on social networking. Facebook was the prime culprit.

http://news.bbc.co.uk/2/hi/technology/6989100.stm

Maybe we should call it social notworking !

The BBC report clarifies this is not a problem unique to the United States. People the world over use these sites, spending time and money on what sure looks like meaningless and maybe voyeuristic behavior.

What about socialization skills? Will this delivery of random information from random sources change the way children learn and make critical judgments?

These are the questions facing our society today. Time will tell whether the implications of this consumer-generated online universe will affect education, journalism, and the national economy.

We know this much: Some Web 2.0 sites have dwindling participation as people drop out of the hype and distraction. Are they moving on to better things, or creating the next new trend? Time will tell.

Benefits of Web 2.0

Is there any redeeming value in Web 2.0?

Of course. There's value in information sharing, having a channel of instant communication, and it is useful even in emergencies.

Additionally...

- Thousands of artists and writers are making money on Web 2.0 and may be unable to afford such visibility otherwise.

- People with disabilities can work from home and fully participate in an online environment.

- Non-profits can maintain visibility with a bigger audience at lower cost with the internet instead of traditional outreach through costly direct mail.

- Web 2.0 provides room for discussion, dialog, and broader access to media than TV & radio.

For a more thorough evaluation of this topic, consider these books:

Everything Is Miscellaneous: The Power of the New Digital Disorder by David Weinberger

The Cult of the Amateur - How Blogs, MySpace, YouTube, and the Rest of Today's User-Generated Media are Destroying Our Economy, Our Culture, and Our Values by Andrew Keen

The Cluetrain Manifesto: The End of Business as Usual by Christopher Locke and Rick Levine.

Ready to sign up?

Facebook & Twitter & LinkedIn, Oh My….

If you want to see what all the hype is about, sign up for free accounts at Facebook.com and Twitter.com. All of the major social media sites are free of charge.

Ask a friend to invite you to join LinkedIn.com. If you offer something useful, and build a following, there's no doubt you could benefit from these sites for fun and networking.

Don't look for me on Twitter –

I'm a Twitter quitter

About ... facebook

Facebook.com acquired over 350 million subscribers
since its launch in 2004. About 100 million are in
the U.S. Users create a page to display their
interests, photos, links to friends. They keep
connected and the population keeps growing, so
exponential growth in friends, networks, and pages
seems unstoppable today. Facebook reports over
50 percent of active users log on in any given day.

Facebook offers tutorials and how-to guides for
publishing and sharing your material.

To get started – just sign up (see next page). You
may wish to use a different email address, so
people who find you on Facebook or any of the
social media sites, won't clog your main email
account. Yahoo Mail and Google's Gmail accounts
have all the storage space you could need.

All the social media sites have useful "Help" files.

Step1. Sign up at facebook.com

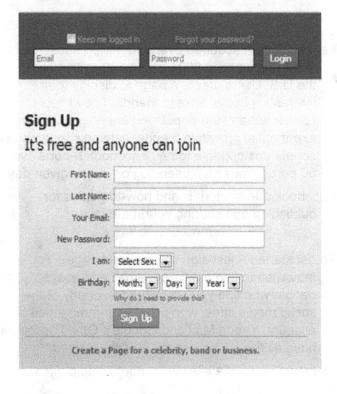

Step 2. Control your settings

Once signed in, you can create your basic profile.
Return to it later if it feels overwhelming, and
consider just how much info you really want to
share publicly. You use "status updates" to type
notes about what you are doing, or to ask a
question to your readers.

Beyond your profile, you can link with friends, use
your Facebook inbox to keep track of people, or
forward the messages to your regular email
address.

Whatever you do or say online is public. Anything
on Facebook can be found by anyone but their
privacy policy states:

"Facebook created public search listings in 2007 to
enable people to search for your name and see a
link to your Facebook profile. They will still only see
a basic set of information."

Settings: Facebook is made up of many linked groups or networks, you can join them, or wait to be invited by friends who notice you're there. You can also visit the Notifications tab under Settings to determine how you want to be notified when someone wants to contact you. There are methods to remind you of birthdays, to sort and share your photos, join groups, and get invited to events.

None of this has to be done when you're first starting out. Take your time, read through other profiles, and add more when you're ready.

Review Facebook's full privacy settings to control your Friends list, and decide which comments and photos should be kept private.

http://www.allFacebook.com/2009/02/Facebook-privacy/

About ... **Linked** in.

Let's get serious now...

One example of a potentially productive business resource is the social media site called linkedin.com.

Remember networking, with "Hello" badges and a handshake? LinkedIn works in a similar way. LinkedIn profile page displays your portfolio, your network, and links to people you know. They become possible connections for your colleagues.

Step1. Sign up at linkedin.com

Your profile at linkedin.com might be more extensive than a public Facebook page, since it connects you with business people and professional affiliations. You can choose to list your current and former employer, work history, education and connections.

Use it to recommend others you've worked with, refer people to sites of interest, invite others to join, and ask for connections.

With LinkedIn, it's not who you know, but who you know who knows someone else. The service is rich with affinity groups, so you can narrow your circle to those with similar interests to yours.

Linked in was formed in 2003. As of December 4, 2009, LinkedIn reports they have over 53 million members across the globe.

About ...

Twitter has really caught on. It is a "micro-blogging" site where users keep in touch with each other by typing short messages (under 140 characters).

The constant stream of people text-messaging (texting) each other seems like a fad that will die quickly. Yet many companies are embracing it as a way to stay in front of their audience.

For quick text messages, Twitter.com seem to have cornered the market for now. Twitter is another free application, but your messages are limited to 140 characters of text. As a result it is referred to as "micro-blogging," with little snippets of what you're up to. For all the friends and followers who track your Twitter name, they instantly see what's going on in your world. Quick twitter messages are called "tweets" and your tweets can automatically appear on Facebook, like status updates, so all your friends can follow you along all day. Of course, if you have 300 friends and they all tweet you all day, you probably won't get much else done.

Sign up at twitter.com

A sample 140-character message:

Twitter is a txt-msg service. U type up 2 140 char of text.
It's ref. to as micro-blogging, cause you kn only post little
snip of what U R doing right now. It kn be hard 2 read.

Now what's the use of this? That's what I wondered,
but in a few short years, Twitter attracts millions of
fans who sure think it's cool. What becomes of
grammar, spelling and punctuation? As you can
see in the sample above, these sites could be
contributing to the great dumbing-down of our
culture.

The Twitter folks say: "Twitter solves information
overload by changing expectations traditionally
associated with online communication. At Twitter,
we ask one question, "What's happening?" The
answers to this question are for the most part
rhetorical. In other words, users do not expect a
response when they send a message to Twitter."

The question you'll soon be asking
yourself:

Who has time to keep up with these sites?

Are they fads that will soon pass?

It's possible, and it's also likely that the
time we have to spend cultivating these
teeny corners of the web might be
better spent elsewhere.

Twitter may be a passing fad, but
something else would quickly take its
place. An industry that supports billions
of dollars in advertising is not without its
value. Twitter is among the firms
looking for a revenue model – a fee-
based system that would make sense,
and somehow add enough value for
users to continue their growth.

About ... You Tube™

YouTube is not exactly a social networking site, where you'd contact someone to make plans for a movie, but plays a strong role in the social, interactive aspects of the web today.

YouTube was founded in 2005, and is now owned by Google. It is the dominant video upload & share community online today.

You might find about 80 percent of the uploaded content to be boring, but the 20 percent with some redeeming value represents an unprecedented opportunity for free promotion for your work and your cause.

YouTube combines social media with audio/video and contains millions of files, viewed daily. The ability to create and upload video directly from cell phones and webcams adds to the popular use.

Using YouTube

As with Facebook and other sites, YouTube has generous "Help" resources in their free online handbook:

http://www.youtube.com/t/yt_handbook_home

Beyond uploading home video, and watching video of concerts, lectures, and loads of funny stuff, like laughing babies, many people use digital cameras to shoot interesting videos, documentaries, and record music. There are bands and performers who got "discovered" by their videos on YouTube. The industry notices when a video gets thousands of clips, and if the content is really good, and the fan base is there, late-night TV can be the next step toward fame.

YouTube reports that 20 minutes of video is uploaded every minute.

And we've all learned that a talented person discovered on "American Idol" or a similar TV program can result in millions of fans almost overnight. As people log onto YouTube and download the music, recording contracts and stardom will follow within weeks, to capture the momentum of sudden celebrity.

There have been "overnight sensations" discovered as long as we've had broadcast radio or television, but now "overnight" literally means what it says. The pace of technology accelerates both good and bad media attention.

So what's the problem with social media?

For starters, it seems to be the tipping point for further dumbing down of America. Culture is reduced to sound bites, people judge the popularity of something based on peer opinion instead of fact. We're seeing a trend toward "consumer journalism," where an eye-witness becomes an expert on national television, because they have a cell phone with a camera. That's not journalism, that's social networking.

Text messaging by typing abbreviated shorthand is not communication. Do we want a generation that can't speak in full sentences, can't form thoughts, can't think independently?

Collectively, popular social media sites are considered an amateur wasteland, and that's probably true for about 70 or 80 percent of the content created.

SOCIAL MEDIA HANDBOOK
Part Two

Five ways to make it work for you:

1. Sign up
2. Control your privacy settings
3. Communication
4. Networking
5. Marketing

Social Media Step 1
Create an account

Whether you're interested in jumping onboard with the social media sites described in this handbook, or are ready to expand your internet use for a site where you can sell art online, join a quilting club, book group, or job search site, it's easy to get started. If you don't like it, you can always unsubscribe from a site, or just stop using it.

To get you started, most online firms require the same basic information. Your real name, a user name and a password.

With adequate anti-virus and spyware protection, you're not at great risk in normal use of the social media sites. Use the same caution in giving our private information as you do elsewhere on the web. Don't click on links that don't look legitimate, and don't "friend" people if it doesn't feel right.

You do not have to accept, or even acknowledge, every "friend" invitation you receive.

Social Media Step 2 Privacy

When you first create an account, don't feel compelled to include all the information requested. Start out by giving only the required data, usually noted by an asterisk, for required fields.

Control your privacy settings by viewing the fine-print before you finish the sign-up process. While you can change your preferences later, some information, once made public, is difficult to retract.

Most online firms have statements like this:

"Review our Privacy Policies to learn more about the kind of data that is collected about you, with whom it is shared, and for what purposes."

Social Media Step 3 Communication

Just as we don't want to forward email jokes to people, we don't want to get stuck in sites that are a waste of time, and lead to loads of other people asking to become our friend. Sometimes we need to escape from the chatter of the world, and these sites can drain both our time and mental clarity.

For most of us, this would seem overwhelming, but if you like technology and you're at the computer, cell phone, iPhone, or Blackberry where you can keep up with the messages and reply, it's a fun way to keep in touch. In fact, it may be cutting down on email overload, since you keep up with these social networking sites on the go.

Social Media Step 3
Communication (con't.)

Perhaps that's better than sitting down at your
    computer at 9 p.m. and finding you have to spend
    an hour weaving through threads of email you
    missed while you were away from the computer.

How to manage your time:

If you visit your Facebook or LinkedIn page daily,
    you'll see an inbox with messages from friends.
    You can also set "Status updates" so you can
    keep people informed of what you're doing, and
    receive their updates.

Have comments emailed to you, if you don't want to
    have to check each site.

And, rather than have an all-consuming involvement
    in social media sites, remember the focus is
    communication. If someone wants to contact you
    on a particular topic, they are more likely do so by
    email or phone, not by leaving a public message.

Social Media Step 4 Networking

Consider the social aspect of 'social media' and use your relationships to network. Networking has always been a powerful tool for business development and for putting people together for mutual benefit.

Examples: Provide job leads, offer suggestions for time-saving strategies, share ideas, introduce your friends to each other.

On Facebook, you could do this by sending a status update or message.

On LinkedIn, you could invite someone into your network.

An effective technique is to cross-promote on each of these sites.

Examples: before writing a blog post, send a Twitter message on the topic to gauge interest. When posted, put it on Facebook, and LinkedIn.

At LinkedIn start a discussion and refer back to the article. Or ask a question seeking an expert opinion on non-profits, and you'll probably receive targeting information.

Social Media Step 4
Networking (con't.)

Remember your LinkedIn page might be seen by professional colleagues and affiliate organizations, while your Facebook page might be viewed by your brother-in-laws wife, who happens to be exactly the person you want to interview for your next feature article.

This is one reason to remember that everything you post online is public. You might make a comment in a Facebook discussion about "the client who's driving you nuts..." only to have that client read your page later, and get the sense that you're talking about her.

It's best to maintain a professional tone in your public posts, and create another site or identity for personal purposes. We've often read of a coach or teacher who lost their job because of photos posted online showing them drinking or caught on-camera goofing around at a party. The worldwide web is truly that, and, for better or worse, its also nearly instant feedback in our lives today.

Social Media Step 5 Marketing

If I had to define the difference between networking and marketing, I'd say:

Networking is widening your circle to reach the most relevant and influential people you can.

Marketing is shining a light on the specific things you do.

Use your contact network to gain business or to promote interest in your organization or group. Instead of heavy-hitting promotion, though, try to provide value for people who are taking the time to read your comments.

Some ideas:

- Offer new information
- Write a helpful article
- Post photos of your products or events
- Suggest five ways to benefit from what you offer
- Highlight the value of volunteering, supporting the local community.

The scope of social media in 2010

Twitter analysts estimate that there are 1.2 million active users, posting more than 2.25 million tweets every day.

http://www.huliq.com/3257/78826/aniston-dumps-mayer-over-twitter-obsession-report

So, is there anything worthwhile on Twitter? Sure. Especially large companies and non-profits who got on board early on. They have learned to send sound-bites out all day, promoting their work or their causes.

Political activism, news sites, and groups such as Nature conservancy are examples you might wish to check out. You'll see a banner like this on most large web sites:

Join The Nature Conservancy on

 flickr

Facebook   Flickr   Twitter

Facebook in perspective

"If Facebook were a country, it would be the eighth most populated in the world, just ahead of Japan, Russia and Nigeria."

Mark Zuckerberg, Facebook co-founder 1/09

While originally a cool tool for teens, Facebook now, according to a Hitwise.com report, shows that the average age of the Facebook user has gone up. Adults between 25 and 44 years old now make up more than half of the social network's user base, up from just 32 percent a year ago.

If teens are backing off because Facebook has lost its cool, advertisers will either change to appeal to older users, or the site may experience further decline.

The state of social media

Astonishing growth rates in social media are
compounded exponentially by expanded
synergies between and among the sites, so
they all claim a growing share of market.

For example: you could use LinkedIn, sending
updates to Facebook, and let people know by
sending a tweet via Twitter and retweet with
status updates all day.

Users can create celebrity fan pages on
Facebook

FriendFeed keeps you busy tracking what your
friends are doing online.

Twitter soared into popularity but, as of this writing, may have reached a peak. A possible decline is indicated by recent stories in the media saying Twitter is flat-lining, and growth has slowed.

Since social media sites all compete for our time, and all can do the same thing: (stay in touch, share music and photos), we may soon see greater convergence.

It seems there is no limit to the capacity of the internet, or of people willing to spend time populating millions of pages with transitory information.

It's doubtful that the volume of services that comprise the existing social media sites will all remain. Until they sort themselves out, though, we will continue to see more innovations, such as a "Flickr2Twitter" service, to share your Flickr photos on Twitter.

Computing chaos?

Remember where the tech industry started.:

    A desire for a computer in every home in America
    Affordable internet access across the country
    An earnest goal to bridge the digital divide.

Enormous research, funding, and resources were used to create the internet, and make high-speed access available around the world.

Then came the flood of information, too much to absorb, leaving us to parse all the data available, and focus on what has meaning for each of us.

It should all come down to something more than chaotic chatter. This technology is likely to improve, so keeping current on technology and cultural trends is one way you can stay informed, aware, and tuned in, to whatever extent you desire.

It's up to you

Just as the social experience varies from person to person – some like rock concerts, others hip-hop. Another group might be private and reclusive.

The third group wants to participate to know what is going on but not become a slave.

A fourth group feels they've got to be there. They were first to have a Wii computer game console, calling it exercise, tweeting on Twitter while getting a haircut, uploading a photo to Facebook so friends could vote on the new haircut.

Just as some people look forward to opera, and others turn off the radio at the first aria, so to, social networking is not for everyone.

If you're on all the social media sites, able to upload video from your cell phone to YouTube, you're a social media star. It's all out there, and for now, it's all free, thanks to advertisers eager to be seen by millions daily. So embrace it. You're part of the "It" generation.

The rest of us are right behind you, waiting to see what happens next.

Notes

Notes

Notes

Notes

Author

Helen Gallagher is national speaker and consultant on publishing and technology. A full presentation on the risks/benefits of using social media sites is available for presentation to your group.

Contact Helen@cclarity.com

Other books by the author:

Release Your Writing
Computer Ease

Helen's business, Computer Clarity, is celebrating over a decade of consulting success with clients around the U.S.
More information is available at www.releaseyourwriting.com.